IF YOU GIVE A
Will He Shut

IF YOU GIVE A KID A COOKIE,
Will He Shut the Fuck Up?

If you give a kid a cookie,

Will he shut the fuck up?

Well, the sugar rush will make him crazy. . . .

So you'll put on a TV show to calm him down,
but a purple dinosaur will tell him scissors are
dangerous. . . .

So he'll reach for a pair,
and knock over your beer.

The smell will remind him of Uncle Billy,
who he'll want to call.

Of course, the old drunk won't answer. . . .

And your kid'll throw a tantrum until you drive over to roust your useless brother-in-law.

On the way, you'll pass a cockfight.

He'll want to stop and watch the birdies. . . .

Then he'll rat you out
for a lollipop,

When a police raid sends you into hiding.

You'll all get thrown in the slammer,

Where he'll scream for mommy.

You'll be bailed out by your wife,
who will hand you divorce papers.

On the way home he'll whine until you play a game. . . .

But peek-a-boo will go horribly wrong.

Back at home he'll light his sister's doll on fire
(just like the convicts taught him).

When you put out the fire . . .

The smoke will remind you and your wife of the rock concert where he was conceived.

You'll start to patch things up but the excitement
will give him a stomachache.

He'll cry hysterically. . . .

And chances are if you
want him to shut the
fuck up,

You'll have to give him a cookie.

Marcy Roznick is a scratch golfer who can curse in over a dozen languages. She also plays the banjo and enjoys knitting trousers. She and her husband live in America with their two sons, whom they love even when they won't shut the f**k up. This is her first book.

Miranda Lemming was born in Amarillo, Texas, and received her schooling through The Cartooning Institute of Detroit. She has had an illustrious career in bumper sticker and t-shirt design. This is her first book.

KID A COOKIE,
the Fuck Up?

Written by Marcy Roznick
Illustrated by Miranda Lemming

 ST. MARTIN'S GRIFFIN ⚞ NEW YORK

M.R.—To Karen, without whom this book would not exist. So blame her.

M.L.—To Jessica, who knows how to make kids behave without a cookie.

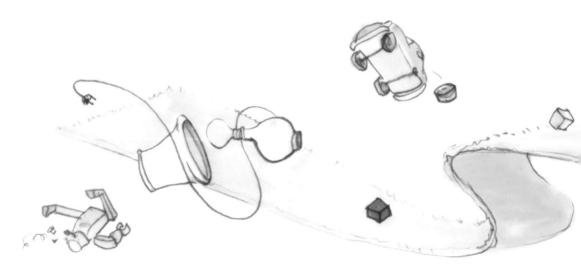

IF YOU GIVE A KID A COOKIE, WILL HE SHUT THE F**K UP? Copyright © 2011 by
Marcy Roznick. All rights reserved. Printed in the United States of America.
For information, address St. Martin's Press, 175 Fifth Avenue, New York, N.Y. 10010.

www.stmartins.com

Illustrations by Miranda Lemming

ISBN 978-1-250-00799-5

First Edition: October 2011

10 9 8 7 6 5 4 3 2 1